Wholeheartedly

Vol I

A Collection of Poems

by

Ra'Shell S. Maldon

GENERAL INFORMATION

"Wholeheartedly"
Vol I

Ra'Shell S. Maldon

All Rights Reserved. No part of this publication may be reproduced, stored in a retrieval system, or transmitted, in any form or in any means – by electronic, mechanical, photocopying, recording or otherwise – without prior written permission of the "Material Owner" or its Representative **B.O.S.S. Publishing, LLC**. Any such violation infringes upon the Creative and Intellectual Property of the Owner pursuant to International and Federal Copyright Law. Any queries pertaining to this "Collection" should be addressed to Publisher of Record.

Copyright © 2021: *Ra'Shell S. Maldon*

Cover Design: *Greg Tellis*

Publisher: *B.O.S.S. Publishing*

Editor: *Terry L. Ware Sr.*

ISBN: *978-0-9988341-4-6*

1. Poetry

First Edition

DEDICATION

Dedicated to anyone who has ever loved and learned life lessons from love (the hard way).

PREFACE

 Wholeheartedly is yet another extension of who I am. It is also a reflection of how I love and how my "third eye" perceives the ones I love. Divided into two parts, this book, much like its predecessor (My Mind's Eye), gives you insight into the most vulnerable aspect of my being (my "fragile" heart). Each part a depiction of two different relationships: the relationship with my estranged male best friend and myself, the relationship with my partner and myself. While reading each poem and each part, I hope you come to understand the power of love.

Whether that love is requited or unrequited, self-love or love for others outside of self, love is a powerful concept, feeling, and (in some instances) drug.

Peace & Positivity,

Ra'Shell Maldon

FOREWORD

Ra'Shell has provided us with another unique look into her life. This unique work opens us up to her actual truth and experiences with relationships and love. A solid reflection that will assist us all in our quest in the attempt to understand the many facets of these two entities that can definitely stand alone.

Fully clear your mind so that you may Wholeheartedly receive what Ra'Shell has for you.

Isaac "Ikegreentea" Crawford

TABLE OF CONTENTS

Dedication |pg. ii

Preface |pg. iii

Foreword |pg. v

Part I: *Loving Him* |pg. **2**

Chapter One:

Queen Reflects King |pg. *3*

Chapter Two:

A Kings Recognition |pg. **6**

Table of Contents.... Continued

Chapter Three:
Checks And Balances |pg. **9**

Chapter Four:
More Checks And Balances |pg. **11**

Part Two: *Loving Her* |pg. **15**

Chapter Five:
Focus |pg. **16**

Chapter Six:
I See You |pg. **19**

Chapter Seven:
I Love You, But… |pg. **22**

Table of Contents.... Continued

Chapter Eight:
Closet Case | pg. **27**

Chapter Nine:
Love by Example | pg. **30**

Chapter Ten:
Better Days Between Us | pg. **35**

Chapter Eleven:
Difference in Priorities | pg. **39**

Chapter Twelve:
Intuitive Flow | pg. **44**

Chapter Thirteen:
Life Decisions | pg. **49**

Chapter Fourteen:
Expendable Me | pg. **54**

Table of Contents.... Continued

Chapter Fifteen:
Bernadine Harris | pg. **57**

Chapter Sixteen:
Losing Myself | pg. **62**

Chapter Seventeen:
Illuminate | pg. **64**

Chapter Eighteen:
Closet Case Part 2 | pg. **68**

Chapter Nineteen:
Inflated Ego | pg. **71**

Chapter Twenty:
S.L.O.W. (Same Loss Old Woe) | pg. **73**

Chapter Twenty-One:
Crew Love | pg. **79**

Table of Contents.... Continued

Chapter Twenty-Two:
This is How She Loses Me | pg. **83**

Chapter Twenty-Three:
S.L.O.W. (Same Loss Old Woe) Part 2 | pg. **86**

Chapter Twenty-Four:
You Against Me | pg. **89**

Chapter Twenty-Five:
Choosing and Losing | pg. **92**

Chapter Twenty-Six:
Together Although Not Together | pg. **96**

Chapter Twenty-Seven:
Burning Bridges | pg. **99**

Chapter Twenty-Eight:
Not Quite There | pg. **101**

Table of Contents.... Continued

Chapter Twenty-Nine:
Home To Homeless | pg. **104**

Chapter Thirty:
I Left | pg. **107**

Table of Contents.... Continued

Author Address | pg. **112**

Author Q&A | pg. **113**

Social Contact | pg. **117**

Wholeheartedly

Vol I

A Collection of Poems

by

Ra'Shell S. Maldon

Wholeheartedly
Vol I

"When the feeling is mutual, it materializes into a bond that's reciprocal."

Wholeheartedly
Vol I

PART I:

LOVING HIM

CHAPTER 1
QUEEN REFLECTS KING

Wholeheartedly
Vol I

This connectivity

Between us

Is so understood it doesn't need

To be explained

To each other nor to any other

Outside of this

So neither of us feels the need

To justify

The meaning

Behind us being the entity

We've evolved into

Reflecting now

On the morning the notion

Began dawning on me

That my very being

Was being

Molded into a reflection of you

And the way you

Conceded to this notion

Wholeheartedly
Vol I

Knowing that I am the softer version of you.

Wholeheartedly
Vol I

CHAPTER 2

A KING'S RECOGNITION

Wholeheartedly
Vol I

Anytime

His presence

Coexists in my present

Its consistency

Serves as a reminder to me consistently

That chivalry isn't dead

Sometimes instead

It lies dormant waiting to be activated

He keeps me elevated

Every time

He draws me in

The way he reads my energy

Anytime

My mind is too opaque

For his third eye to see through

Every time

I feel invisible

His actions

And his words utter with conviction

Wholeheartedly
Vol I

In unison

I…see…you.

CHAPTER 3
CHECKS AND BALANCES

Wholeheartedly
Vol I

Whenever he

Senses my actions

Are finding complacency

With contradicting my words

He has the tendency

To use my words

Against me

Saving me from hypocrisy

While reassuring me that he is indeed listening

Whenever I speak.

CHAPTER 4
MORE CHECKS AND BALANCES

Wholeheartedly
Vol I

We take turns

Being the voice of reason

When it is my turn

I offer him the multitude of lessons

That I continuously

Gain guidance and clarity from

And I sow

These seeds of positivity and productivity

For him to reap

So that I do not feel the need to be

In his present nor his presence

In order to be

Certain that he heeds

To my forewarnings in his present

Because ultimately

The outcome

Is always apparent

And his soul

Is always as transparent

Wholeheartedly
Vol I

As his intentions

Seem to be.

"When the feeling is one-sided, any bond that binds is unequally divided and lopsided."

Wholeheartedly
Vol I

PART II:

LOVING HER

CHAPTER 5

FOCUS

Wholeheartedly
Vol I

Temptation is almost always there

And I pretend often

To be unaware

Of its existence

Only because I never care

That it exists

Even when I am not inside

Of my woman I still feel her energy there

As if her love follows me

Any and everywhere

Steadily

That feeling

Vibrates

Within my being

Moving my soul like a soulful melody

Until it finally

Radiates

On the outside of me

Profusely

Wholeheartedly
Vol I

Seeping through my pores

As my heart instinctively closes any revolving doors

Denying access to new lust

And old love

While simultaneously setting the foundation for trust.

Wholeheartedly
Vol I

CHAPTER 6

I SEE YOU

Wholeheartedly
Vol I

My three eyes see you

Even when your thoughts are too opaque

To see through

And they see

Over, under, and straight through

The guard you seem to

Build around your every vulnerability

Still my three eyes see you

As easily as

If you are a misguided extension of me

And knowing you

To the extent that I do

I know that you deserve so much more

Than the little to nothing

You find yourself settling for

Although I cannot be sure

Whether you are settling

Because your past keeps meddling

In your present

Wholeheartedly
Vol I

Or because you underestimate

Yourself

So, you miscalculate

Your worth

For what it is worth

I see royalty underneath the surface of you

A queen in my three eyes

I see through

Your façade to the real you

Even if your view

Is far too obscured for you to see in yourself

Everything that I see in you.

Wholeheartedly
Vol I

CHAPTER 7

I LOVE YOU, BUT...

Wholeheartedly
Vol I

If your heart could talk

I imagine this to be

The thought

It would convey to me

Undoubtedly

I know it would say

I love you, but

I won't allow myself to commit to you

And I hate to

Sound cliché, but

With conviction allow me to say

It's not you

It's me

In a solo state of mind

Is currently where I seem to be

And although I've suffered through

All the hurt

I'm afflicting upon you

Wholeheartedly
Vol I

Not even that seems to be enough to

Encourage me to

Break the cycle of hurt people

Hurting people too

Unfortunately

For you

Rarely do we commit to

Anyone or anything outside of us

Romantically

I know you desire trust,

But I'm untrustworthy and transparency

Isn't a must

For me

I've found comfort in the complacency

Of duplicity and secrecy

Still I love you, but

I know I may never be ready

To give you

Wholeheartedly
Vol I

The little that you

Ask of me

Like my honesty

Because I'm honestly

Too distracted with giving a fraction

Of me to everybody

So, I rarely notice the lack of reciprocity

Or the little attention and energy

I give to you

Still I love you, but

I won't give you my undivided anything

I'm too selfish

And I doubt I'll ever gift you

With a promise ring,

An engagement ring, or anything

That solidifies your place

With me publicly

And I know you desire monogamy, but

Wholeheartedly
Vol I

I'm too unsettled to settle

Down with you

Although I appreciate everything

For me that you do

And although I love you,

Sometimes I still need the space

To give my love to other lovers outside of you.

Wholeheartedly
Vol I

CHAPTER 8
CLOSET CASE

Wholeheartedly
Vol I

She hides her habit

Frequently

Out of habit

From those who couldn't fathom

Our frequency

Or from those who habitually

Undermine

These life choices of hers and mine

Her actions

Often leave me behind

Feeling as if I have a fraction

Of her

Now I wonder

If she'll ever be as free spirited as me

And if she'll ever regard me

Publicly

As she does when we're in private

And the outside world

Fades then becomes radio silent

Wholeheartedly
Vol I

Or perhaps she perceives my presence in her world

As temporary as the blue in my hair

Or the red in her eyes

Easily hidden

And just as easily forgotten.

CHAPTER 9
LOVE BY EXAMPLE

Wholeheartedly
Vol I

My woman knows

That I love her

She even knows

That she loves me

Even though

She doesn't quite know

Whether she is or isn't in love with me

And even though

She doesn't quite know

How to love

Nor how to be loved

Wholeheartedly

Something inside of me

Compels me to love her still

As if she were an extension of me

But the way she reacts to

Then retracts from me

Leads me to believe

Wholeheartedly
Vol I

That I love her in a way

Her exes couldn't ever conceive

But perhaps intended

Although they couldn't achieve

Instead they left her unattended with her heart dented

Scarred and marred

Seemingly beyond my ability to repair

I swear

Still I love her

With such an intensity

That my love for her glows

Bright so that even the blindest being

Can see it

And my love for her flows

Deep so that even the most insensitive being

Can feel it

I love her this way

In hopes that her past heartache may

Someday be

Wholeheartedly
Vol I

A distant memory

And her past wounds

Maybe closed then sealed

Never to reopen

But forever healed solely

So that maybe

She may love herself

Then allow herself to love someone else

Outside of her wholly

Even if that someone isn't me

I simply want her

To not only

Understand but also

I want her to know

The authenticity

And the simplicity of real love

As well as its ability

To outgrow

Wholeheartedly
Vol I

Past pain endured during heartache's reign.

CHAPTER 10
BETTER DAYS BETWEEN US

Wholeheartedly
Vol I

She

Gives to me

Any materialistic thing

Without regards to the cost

As if to her money isn't anything

More than a loss

To reup from

Adding winnings to earnings

That we count up then count down

As we deduct from

Paying bills

Before rotating the wheels

That lead us away

From distraction

And closer to

Regaining more than a fraction

Of each other

But wholly

Solely

Wholeheartedly
Vol I

Seeking to forget

The obstacles holding us back

And reconnect

That's every getaway for two

In which we roam

For a day

Or two

Or for a weekend and a weekday

She

Habitually spoils me in her own way

With shopping sprees

Anything that she buys

For herself she

Also buys

For me

At shopping outlets out of town

Or an outlet that's somewhere out of state

No matter the destination

Wholeheartedly
Vol I

No matter the time

And no matter the date

She

Makes reservations

For two

Reserving for us one of the finest suites

With some of the nicest views

And the softest sheets

With minimal regard for the nightly rate

All so we

Can dine in various places amongst unfamiliar faces

While sipping various drinks to chase

The taste of leftover appetizers and entrees once hot now going cold on our plates.

CHAPTER 11
DIFFERENCE IN PRIORITIES

Wholeheartedly
Vol I

I hate that I have to remind you

Of all the things I've done

And continue to do

For you

And for the family

That you casually invited me into

Under false pretense

Leaving my fragile heart in suspense

As you recklessly dispense

Your attention, energy, and riches

Chasing disloyal, disrespectful bitches

Who don't respect themselves

Enough to respect you

Let alone respect the woman you come home to

Every night

Then awake with every morning

And that's so far from right

It's wrong

How easily they carry on

Wholeheartedly
Vol I

Disrespecting another woman's home

As though

They devalue the notion of family

Unlike me

Who foolishly values our family

More so than you

This is evident in the way

That I reprioritize

My needs so that our family's needs

Are met

And how I disregard any outside distractions

So that you have me

Wholeheartedly not merely a fraction

Without any misdirection

When it comes to my perception

Of knowing the difference between options and priorities

Because in my eyes

It makes sense that our family

Come before anything

Wholeheartedly
Vol I

So, I put them over everything

Despite the way that you adamantly

Leave us behind

Temporarily

Out of sight and out of mind

As you continuously

Neglect and disrespect our home steadily

Placing temporal things

Like money

And lust

Ahead of sacred things

Like family,

Real love, and trust

As if the latter

Should never outrank the former

Or as if the importance

Of prioritizing in a specific order doesn't matter.

CHAPTER 12
INTUITIVE FLOW

Wholeheartedly
Vol I

Living the naked truth

Never hurts more

Than existing in a dressed-up lie

We both know to be

A stretch from our reality

And if my father can look at me

Dead in the eye

Then speak a straight-faced lie

With conviction

And without apology

Then how much weight can your contradictory diction

Possibly hold to me

Unlike you

Who seems to be too preoccupied to read me

Somehow, I always seem to read you

As clear as day

Reading between the lines

Of any and everything

Wholeheartedly
Vol I

You do or do not say

Because your language of body

Speaks volumes to me

Even louder than your voice

Which never seems to be filled with remorse

Nor regret

For the disrespectful acts you commit

Habitually

Meanwhile pushing me

Emotionally and mentally out of the way

As you physically

Navigate your way

Carelessly

Running back to the toxicity

Of your past

As you cast away the stability

I provide for a part of your history

That was never built to last

Longer than a season

Wholeheartedly
Vol I

Still you can't provide a reason

For finding complacency

In reverting back to old habits

That never seem to die

Mainly because you never seem to try

To bury them deeper than just beneath the surface

Still I never need to wait

For the wrong you do in the dark

To come to the light

Because like clockwork

Your wrongdoing always works

It way to the surface

Serving no other purpose

Other than stroking

Your inflated ego

While serving you a taste of familiarity

At the expense of losing me.

Wholeheartedly
Vol I

CHAPTER 13
LIFE DECISIONS

Wholeheartedly
Vol I

Should we civilly

Discuss this ginormous

Elephant that's been lurking awkwardly

In the common rooms

Or no?

Should we just leave it be

Until eventually

We lock then unload

Our frustrations

And implode before we explode

Unleashing the pain

While releasing the build-up

Or should we just

Let it go?

Really, I don't know

It's been some odd days

In a row

Wholeheartedly
Vol I

Of navigating through the maze

In my mind's eye

While avoiding eye-to-eye contact

And conversation

With endurance to withstand

The awkward silence

In which we now stand

Only to await

The coexistence

Of uncertainty and mistrust

And create

A consistent rift

Between us

That inconsistently shifts.

This is her heart's history on repeat

An unbroken cycle

That skips every other beat,

But never breaks.

Wholeheartedly
Vol I

Navigating her way out of the friend zone

Has proven to be

Another one of those mistakes

I seem to make

Every time

I fall head over heels

In the very thing

That kills

Me softly then stills

Me every time

Right before it heals me only to repeat

Her habit of self-sabotage

Will ultimately be our defeat.

So, should we see this love as the mirage

It really is?

And should we end this sooner

Rather than later?

Should the decision be now or never

Or from now until forever?

Wholeheartedly
Vol I

Even though we're dodging the sight

Of ultimatums left and right

For whatever reason,

Should we accept that our situation-ship

Has long sailed

And long-lived its season

After it aborted another mission failed?

CHAPTER 14

EXPENDABLE ME

Wholeheartedly
Vol I

Is she going to pull me

Deeper into her?

Or is she going to push me

Further away?

Honestly, it's difficult for me to say

For sure

Especially when her

Actions always contradict her words

As though when it comes to us she is indecisively unsure

Like whenever she says she needs me

But then carries on

As though she needs her past crutch more

And I carry on

As though I could possibly compete

Spending countless hours

Chasing after a piece of her heart

Until my feet

Feel sore

Only to find myself breathless

Wholeheartedly
Vol I

And hopelessly

Searching the depths of my heart for

Answers to questions

Like what am I still here for?

Spending countless minutes

Wondering whether she is loyal to me

Or whether her loyalty

Remains divided between her history and me?

Or whether my focus should be

Less on us

And more on me?

: Wholeheartedly
Vol I

CHAPTER 15
BERNADINE HARRIS

Wholeheartedly
Vol I

Maybe it's my heart's frailty

Or maybe its gullibility

Shielding me

From truly seeing

That my very being is being

Reconstructed around a dream

Sold to me by the

One person I trust, love,

And place above

My own selfish needs

Giving you the best of me selflessly

Without seeking reciprocity

Only seeking to love you

Wholeheartedly

While demonstrating to you

How to love me

Yet here I am still lacking

And there you are still stacking

Your selfish reasons

Wholeheartedly
Vol I

For being misleading before leaving me

In the company

Of misery

An act of personal treason

Against a heart

Mistakenly align with yours

Despite how I tirelessly play my part

Day after day

It's unsettling how easily

You stray away

From home leaving me all alone

Without a clue

Of the duplicitous things you do

And despite everything for you that I do

Or everything I am

And I have been to you

I can't help but fear

Wholeheartedly
Vol I

My undoing is drawing near

Alongside our oncoming demise

Resulting from your inability to compromise

Still I search hopelessly

For a sign of forever

Within your eyes

But my weary eyes can never

Seem to find it

Instead whenever

I look into you I am blatantly reminded

Of our reality

No longer are you in love with me

And no longer do you see me

As you once did

Still I can't seem to find the strength to rid

My heart of its love for you

So, I foolishly stand by your side

Oblivious to the wandering heart dwelling inside you.

Wholeheartedly
Vol I

Wholeheartedly
Vol I

CHAPTER 16
LOSING MYSELF

Wholeheartedly
Vol I

Habitually
I exerted so much of my energy
Into learning you
That I lost sight of me
And mistakenly
Overrode my identity
In order to fit the perception of me
That you cared to see.

CHAPTER 17
ILLUMINATE

Wholeheartedly
Vol I

She finds difficulty

In disconnecting from the world

But she finds it easy to disconnect from me

Even though I offer her

Realness and clarity

She reminds me

That she finds comfort in the complacence

Of her own ignorance

Along with the company of misery too

She remains a misguided tool

A drunken fool

Stumbling in a dark place

Without a trace

Of light

Well, that's not quite true

Because she has me

And although my soul shines bright

My light wasn't quite enough to shine through

As if her pride shaded her view

Wholeheartedly
Vol I

And it wasn't quite enough to guide her astray

From her wrongs then redirect her in the way of her rights

For she avoids any sight

Of the truth even when it's hiding in plain sight

As if it might

Not ever catch up to her

As if my light won't somehow will transparency

From her whether voluntarily

Or involuntarily

So that I might be able to see

Straight through her

But to my chagrin

She remains adamant about being opaque as can be

As she once again

She carries her demons like accessories

As if she's afraid to exist in this world without them.

CHAPTER 18

CLOSET CASE PART 2

Wholeheartedly
Vol I

This love seems idle

At times it comes with unspoken titles

And without any

Publicized symbols of commitment

Like tattoos, rings,

Or anything

Leaving me to find

That none of her friends or family

Know me

To them I am a nobody

Wait…no

Let me rephrase

To them I am a faceless somebody

Who is always around

Still none of them know me

To them I am merely another female homie

Or maybe they perceive me

Wholeheartedly
Vol I

To be just another fickle fling

That may never amount to anything more

Than her foot out the door

Of another seemingly meaningless situation-ship.

CHAPTER 19
INFLATED EGO

Wholeheartedly
Vol I

You so eagerly

Leave your lady

Home alone and waiting

Tossing and turning between the sheets

Of a bed once shared

By she and you

But now no longer occupied by two

Just one warm body

Her without you

All so you can run the streets

Giving chase

At a steady pace

To your ex-bae then your potential next bae

And whomever else may

Give you the attention your ego

Desperately

Needs to feed off of to survive.

CHAPTER 20

S. L. O. W.

(SAME LOSS OLD WOE)

Wholeheartedly
Vol I

It seems that she was her first everything

And I wasn't her first anything

Although

She broke her heart

And she also played a part in her family

Being torn apart

Along with her self-esteem

Although

She always treated her like property

And she habitually

Degraded her

And often acted as if she hated her

She was always queen to me

So there was nothing

Except love

Given from me to her

So consistently

I reconstructed her frown

In a way

Wholeheartedly
Vol I

That made her smile

More

And I aligned my actions with my words

In a way

That made her feel secure

Before and after she lost it all

All the while

I preserved the energy that sustained me

As I travelled the extra to mile

And demonstrated the extent of my love for her

By the way I took care

Of her

Wants and needs

Whenever she found herself

In want or in need

Of anything

Even on my longest day

I would slay

A homecooked meal in the kitchen

Wholeheartedly
Vol I

Before and after I would lay

Her yoni to rest in the bedroom

Still despite

How I truly adored her

And despite

All that I have done for her

I still haven't received a ring or anything

Meaningful from her

That solidified a commitment to me

Because apparently

Her heart wasn't truly with me

It's still being manipulated

And abated

By the grown girl who

Broke her in

Then

Broke her down

But who

Didn't lend a hand

Wholeheartedly
Vol I

Even when she needed a helping hand around

To sustain

Herself and to maintain

Her household

In the midst of her darkest hours

Yet I was there

Consistently

Ready and willing as I showered

Her for hours

With all of the adoration and affection

Her soul could withstand

I built her up then held her down

And stood my ground

Until her actions and words conveyed

That she no longer wanted

Nor needed my existence around

Because she apparently

Preferred being with her first everything

More so than anything

Wholeheartedly
Vol I

She ever established with me.

Wholeheartedly
Vol I

CHAPTER 21

CREW LOVE

Wholeheartedly
Vol I

A year from where we started

We're still

Where we started

Her getting her feel and getting a thrill

From playing house

While also playing the field

As for me

I'm trying to deal with the feel

Of being brokenhearted

From habitually

Being spoon-fed a serving of lies

Smothered in secrecy

Meant for covering up old ties

She pretends

To sever or she tends

To downplay

Meanwhile I'm still

Analyzing every word she thinks to say

Along with the way

Wholeheartedly
Vol I

Her language of body

Speaks to me

As I seemingly

Digest them and ingest small doses of the truth

Laced with enough intuition

To give me indigestion

Every time I ignore the proof

Always hiding

In plain sight

Although physically anchored here

This fragile heart

Aches to disappear

Mentally getting lost in the thought

Of taking flight

Emotionally too weary

To continue to put up a fight

For a love that wasn't meant for me

But it was seemingly

Meant to be

Wholeheartedly
Vol I

Divided unevenly

Among myself

And everyone who came prior to me

As if I haven't earned

Seniority.

Wholeheartedly
Vol I

CHAPTER 22
THIS IS HOW SHE LOSES ME

Wholeheartedly
Vol I

History

Has a tendency

Of repeating itself if

There's a lesson to receive

But the recipient isn't inclined to retrieve it

The first time around

And although I offered her

A life vest

To help her

Find rest

And to stay afloat she rejected it

As if she would rather continue to drown

In her lust

For chasing selfish wants

And misusing trust,

As she continuously puts an ingenuous

Woman down

In order to lift a disingenuous

Grown girl up.

CHAPTER 23

S. L. O. W. (SAME LOSS OLD WOE) PART 2

Wholeheartedly
Vol I

She couldn't view

The presence of a blessing

In her present

She was far too

Preoccupied clinging to a five year long

Part of her past

Although the attraction is strong

I doubt the universe intended that affair to last

Longer than the season

It took to leave destruction in its wake

I often wonder

How long it will take

For her to wander

Astray from continuously

Deciding to relive the same mistake

Of mistaken

Infatuation with love

While simultaneously

Setting those undeserving on a pedestal high above

Wholeheartedly
Vol I

The one deserving

Of anything and everything she has to offer

For the reason

It seems she prefers pretending to be available

Over actually being committed

And available

To anyone fitted

Between her and the past

She may never cast

Aside

Whether out of

Pride

Or pure stupidity

For stupidly

Believing that she doesn't deserve something

And someone

Better than she has always almost had.

Wholeheartedly
Vol I

CHAPTER 24
YOU AGAINST ME

Wholeheartedly
Vol I

You always take things too far

Much like the driver

Of a car

Being driven aimlessly

You shamelessly

Show me the extent of your cruelty

As you mentally

And emotionally

Bully me

Until I implode

Then explode violently

Releasing everything built up inside of me

Much like the bullied

Standing up for the first time to the bully

Without fully

Contemplating the consequence

Of retaliation

Then without hesitation and with much concentration

Your thoughtless words cut into me

Wholeheartedly
Vol I

Simultaneously

As your hatred filled eyes

Bore through me.

CHAPTER 25
CHOOSING AND LOSING

Wholeheartedly
Vol I

By now I should be

Used to dealing

With lovers as indecisive as you

And by now I should be

Used to feeling

As insignificant as I do

In your world at times whenever

It comes to you

Instead in the presence of you

My emotions are reeling

Although my facial expression is revealing

Forced nonchalance

My eyes betray me by revealing

The weariness

Brought on by the negligence

And the ignorance

Driving her to habitually

Chase after her past

As if

Wholeheartedly
Vol I

That once hidden affair was ever intended to last

Or as if

Being a mistress

Is more meaningful than being a wife

Or as if

Clinging to her mistress

Is more meaningful than living a monogamous life

Even though she knows her past

Would cast her aside

Just as fast

As it reels her in on a whim of its choosing

Her heart is all I want

And although she periodically flaunts

It before me

I'm consistently losing

Because she's never

Choosing me

Over anything except a lonely night

And always

Wholeheartedly
Vol I

Against my better judgement

Back to her

I come running chasing after

Her heart

Only as an afterthought

The morning after

Being caught in the rapture

Of touching her bean from late night

Until early morning.

CHAPTER 26
TOGETHER ALTHOUGH NOT TOGETHER

Wholeheartedly
Vol I

Although

We are often together

I know

We are not together

Rather

We are both free to do whatever

With our downtime

With whomever

We see fit to find time for

As though we have not weathered

The stormiest of weather

Together

Or as though I have not remained

A steady anchor

Holding her steadily

In the midst of the roughest sea

No we are not together

I am merely the heart of this entity

That we somehow grew to be

Wholeheartedly
Vol I

Despite the reality

That no we are not together

No matter how often we appear to be.

CHAPTER 27
BURNING BRIDGES

Wholeheartedly
Vol I

Watching the memories

Of our history

Dwindle into nothing more than soot

Found at the foot

Of an ashtray

Fully aware of the root cause

That drives this bridge between her and me

To burn without pause

But not before these memories

Dance in the shade

Of the flames

Until they inevitably fade

Away

To wherever the smoke may settle.

CHAPTER 28

NOT QUITE THERE

Wholeheartedly
Vol I

Even though

I would like to be in a place where

I no longer care

To know

And no longer care

About where

It is that she may go

Or who it is she may be with

When am I not around

And even though

I know

Knowing and caring is only brining me down

I know

I am nowhere near

That place

Where I can be comfortable

Granting her space

To do the duplicitous things in the light

And in my face

Wholeheartedly
Vol I

That she has always done in the dark

Behind my back.

Wholeheartedly
Vol I

CHAPTER 29

HOME TO HOMELESS

Wholeheartedly
Vol I

I had it all

And I left it all

Behind

Except the son she gifted me

I couldn't leave him

Behind

To be raised singlehandedly

By someone who lives life so irresponsibly

The boy is mine

So when we voluntarily

Left our home

Behind

I was seeking to find

Solace

And a peace

Of mind for us both

As well as

A loving environment for our continued growth

But I found neither

Wholeheartedly
Vol I

Inside our home nor outside of it either

Which left me to wonder

Why

Do I continue to wander

From one broken home to the next.

Wholeheartedly
Vol I

CHAPTER 30

I LEFT

Wholeheartedly
Vol I

I surrendered to the discouragement

That encouraged me

To leave my home and coexist uncomfortably

In the home of another

Although

I know

I am justified in leaving

My logic is incessantly seething

That maybe

I shouldn't have left

But I left

Thinking that my absence

Might have a greater impact than my presence

I left

Thinking that leaving was the right

Move for me to make

To redirect my energy in the direction

Of a peace of mind

And a consistent connection

Wholeheartedly
Vol I

To whomever awaits me whenever I come home

But I left

Without knowing the difficulty

Of staying away

Because I left

Without knowing that the home

I sought refuge in

Is as broken as the home

I left

And I cannot begin

To repair

The irreparable damage

Done here

So the longer I stay

The more it becomes crystal clear

That my existence has no place coexisting anywhere

Except the place

Spacious enough to house my baggage and me

Somewhere

Wholeheartedly
Vol I

I can be free to organize and throw

Away said baggage

At my own pace in the comforts of my own space

With room to grow.

Wholeheartedly
Vol I

AUTHOR'S
CORNER

Wholeheartedly
Vol I

Wholeheartedly
Vol I

AUTHOR'S ADDRESS

Dear Reader,

Self-love can be a difficult process. One filled with a combination of trial and error as well as trial and triumph. When you learn to master self-love, loving someone or something outside of yourself is as easy as breathing or blinking. Be warned... love is easy to acquire, but hard to maintain. And loving is a process... accept it, embrace it, and evolve with it. It, being love.

Peace & Positivity,

Ra'Shell S. Maldon

Wholeheartedly
Vol I

AUTHOR'S Q&A

Q: What ever happened to my relationship with him?

A: *We grew apart, but we cross paths every now and again.*

Q: What do I miss and love about him?

A:

1. His realness (He was as real with me as I was with him.)
2. His conversation
3. His outlook
4. His soul

Q: Why did I decide to stay... with her?

Wholeheartedly
Vol I

A:

1. Love (for her and her children)
2. Attachment (to her children)
3. Stability
4. Need

Q: Why did I decide to leave…her?

A:

1. Lack of respect
2. Lack of reciprocity
3. **Infidelity**
4. **Selfishness**
5. **Unwillingness to change**

Q: What do I miss and love about her?

Wholeheartedly
Vol I

A:

1. ***Her affection***
2. ***Her compassion***
3. *Her friendship*
4. *Her sense of humor*

Q: Will I continue or discontinue my relationship with her children?

A: As much as I love them, and as much as I miss them, I am uncertain whether I can or will be able to continue being a part of their lives.

Q: Am I still a hopeless romantic and do I hope real love will find me someday?

A: Against my better judgement...I am and I do.

Q: What do I want?

A:

1. *Respect*
2. *Transparency*

3. *Recognition*

4. *Monogamy*

5. *Commitment*

6. *Longevity*

Q: What do I need?

A: *A helpmeet who loves himself enough to respect and reciprocate the love I give.*

Wholeheartedly
Vol I

SOCIAL CONTACT

Raapostrophe.blogspot.com

.

.

.

.

Twitter.com/raapostrophe

.

.

.

Instagram.com/raapostrophe

www.ingramcontent.com/pod-product-compliance
Lightning Source LLC
Chambersburg PA
CBHW070502100426
42743CB00010B/1724